I0201712

Living From The Inside Out

Experiencing Unending Joy in Life

by

Olu Sobanjo

LIVING FROM THE INSIDE OUT
Experiencing Unending Joy in Life

ISBN-13: 978-0-9781595-2-8
© 2014 by Olu Sobanjo

All rights reserved.

Published by Afropages

Kingston, Ontario, Canada.

www.olusobanjo.com

Printed in USA.

Dedication

To the one who gave me unending joy. I am
lost for words to describe what I experience as I come
into your presence daily. From the moment I got to
know the new life I have in you, to this day, my life has
not been the same.

Thank you dear Lord for giving my life a whole new
meaning.

I am yours Lord!

Acknowledgements

This is the first book I have published and I am thrilled to have enjoyed the help and support of everyone far and near.

- My life has been shaped by countless hours of discussion with my dear friend, husband and boss, Ade. Thanks for your input into this book. I will never repay you for your leadership and love. Thanks for allowing me to be myself for these many years. It has been a blessing serving God beside you.

- To my 2 wonderful sons, Demi and Damilola, Thanks for your understanding while I needed some silence around the house and for constantly asking when the book will be out. Here it is!

- To Andrea Flutsch for your weekly reminder to work on the book.

- To my dear sister (in-law) Dr. Bola, for your friendship and for always being available to edit my work.

- To everyone that God has added to my life through Overcomers Assembly, thank you for teaching me to follow God daily. And especially to every lady that has worked with me to organize Vessels of Gold Conference since 2007, you all have added so much to me and I am really grateful to be your friend.

- To my mom, Evang. Grace Olowosoyo who has been a great inspiration to me as long as I have lived. Love you mom.

- To my Dad, Pa. John Akin. Olowosoyo, I am grateful to God for each moment of your training. I am still your Ajenje!

- To my Brothers & sisters, thanks for your candid opinion and love always.

- And to my amazing Parents (in-law) for your support and love always. I am so grateful to have you both in my life.

- To everyone that has given me the opportunity of personally mentoring them, thank you. I am eternally grateful to God for you. And I want to continue to learn through you.

- Finally, to all my friends and family members all over the world. Thanks. I pray that you all will thrive in life daily. God bless you all.

Table of Content

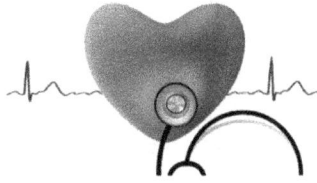

Introduction

In Christianity today, many learn to say the truths before they believe it and therefore many speak the truth without experiencing the truth in their own lives. You know how the gospel goes: 'all your sins are forgiven'. Wow! Anyone who believes that would get excited enough to want to share with others, so what happens next is that many of these people learn to share with others what they have heard about Jesus before they work hard to pursue and befriend the Jesus that did such a great thing for them.

These people go around sharing with others a truth that they themselves have not experienced personally. Hence, we have many in the church today that are there because they were convinced to choose Jesus as their insurance policy for life after death. As much as this is true, there is more to what Jesus came to do here on earth than saving us from hell.

Others are frustrated because they are only repeating what others say, deep down they are not sure it has any depth at all. Why? Because while they have been reciting the scripture and memorizing it, it has not changed their situation. The person that told them about Christ said, "Receive Jesus and receive joy and peace". They received Jesus but are still awaiting joy and peace. Some have even said, "I don't think it's working for me," and they have gotten responses like, "weeping may endure for the night but joy comes in the morning" and "a thousand years is like a day before God." Oh my, who wants to wait a thousand years before receiving joy and peace? Many have been advised to keep holding on to faith in the word of God, never give up, and run away from sin. The list goes on.

The thief comes only in order to steal and kill and destroy. I came that they may have and enjoy life, and have it in abundance (to the full, till it overflows) John 10:10 AMP.

In this book I want to demonstrate a simple way to approach the work that Jesus did and how that applies to you. It's my desire that after reading this booklet, you will have a desire to completely pursue a full time (an on-going) relationship with the life giving savior and lord, Jesus. Jesus' promise of abundant life is the basis for this book.

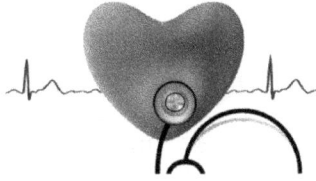

1

Are You Adopted?

Many devout church members are devoted to their churches because they hope to enjoy more blessings in their lives and family. (If I serve God faithfully may be He will solve the problems in my life.) Many have become faithful members of the Church even before meeting the Christ who owns the family.

If you are a parent you know that your child would invite his /her friend home as much as you allow. However that does not make the other child become your son/daughter. This can only happen if you personally go through the process of adoption. In order words, they must have a personal relationship with you, not just your child. Of course they can have a very close relationship with your child; they can stay over and even get to know all your relatives.

This reminds me of a situation between myself and one of my very good friends. She entered into my life when I was in the last year of primary (elementary) school. Her parents were new in town. We attended the same church and we became very good friends. We had play dates almost every weekend with sleepover privileges and, funny enough, our last names were very similar.

Not only were we very close to each other, people around also began to see us as the same. We sang duets together at church among many other things. Because of our closeness, she knew members of my extended family as much as I knew members of hers.

However, though we were very close (and still are), I never became a legal member of her family and she did not become a member of mine. Both of our parents love our friendship and they did many things to demonstrate this to us, but they did not decide to adopt the other child because of our closeness. In other words they did not take on the responsibility of being the parents by signing a document to become my friends' dad and mom and vice versa.

Assuming that there was a need for either of us to become adopted into the other family, a meeting would have been necessary to discuss the options. Then forms would have to be completed by the adopting parent, with some necessary consent from other family members so the process could become final, with the government also playing a role. Then the relationship begins in a new way. Friends become sisters and so on. Before an adoption can take place, there must be a transaction between the parent and the child to be.

In many cases, when someone hears the message they accept it by faith and accept what they were told without making further efforts to meet the Jesus behind the message. Sadly, people that do not see their need for Jesus (at all) are living in his home and are expecting things to change in their lives suddenly.

Many Christians are unfulfilled; they do not enjoy their lives in Christ because they have not taken time to get to know Jesus himself and what he did for them. You will see this set of people looking for more by attending any event that promises them more. In their subconscious they are looking for the next big thing that might bring the fulfillment they so desperately need. They run towards every opportunity for a new experience in God. Deep down they are hoping that the new minister will be able to show them or even give them a cure to the emptiness they feel within.

Many of such are referred to as hypocrites by others; they act right but on the inside are so confused and frustrated, which causes them to be defeated or even sometimes grow wicked. These people also assume that many Christians are like them so they might not even see any reason for a real change.

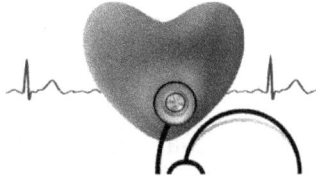

2

That Was Me

This idea is very important to me because for many years, I was at this point myself. I gave my life to the Lord as a teenager but did not really know how to pursue a personal relationship with Christ. I studied the bible and prayed and was careful to study everything I needed to know. Sadly, my main concern was not to know Jesus Christ my Lord, to understand what he did for me and then live my life totally for him. My aim on the other hand was to shine brightly so that the world may know that I am a child of God.

You might wonder what was wrong with my focus. All I wanted was to know His word and pray a lot in order to build spiritual muscles to become like one of the spiritual giants I saw around. The problem was I was not pursuing Jesus as a friend and Lord. I was pursuing the person I could become because of what he did for me. I saw more of what I needed to be to help the church; to look like other vibrant Christians; and to know what they were doing.

I was so confused that I thought I needed to have my devotions daily in order to be a good Christian, I prayed for long hours because that's what you do to grow. I fasted weekly and did many spiritual acts in order to become a better vessel in God's hands. I grew more in the area of my service to God and not so much in the area of my personal relationship with Jesus. I liken my growth at the time to that of a wheat stem. With a little bit of pressure you could uproot a wheat plant unlike an apple tree that requires more effort to be uprooted.

I desired to hear God all the time despite only making real efforts when I had major decisions to make. On the surface I was one of the nice Christian ladies you see around but deep down my Christianity was pretty much shallow. I cared a lot about what people thought about me so I only worked hard to be seen as a good Christian.

I used to buy sermon tapes to learn more about God. I enjoyed listening to very insightful sermons in order to know what else I could do for or share with others about this great God. However only the surface of my heart was being changed. I saw myself as a good Christian and could not assess the state of my own heart. Why? Because I was not looking inside.

Many people are like this today. They pursue human achievements and standards. They always fuel their heart with worship music; they are always at every church event. They even try out other churches with the intention of discovering another revelation from God. But they never settle down to check their own heart.

God allows different situations and people into our lives that will help draw attention to our heart. Most of the time, we try to fix these situations by praying to get rid of the issue. For instance, a Christian lady is faced at work with someone that obviously does not like her; this person begins to stress her. The question is this, is it the devil that is bringing persecution to a Christian in this example or is it God that allowed the persecution in order to get her attention to check the state of her own heart?

Years ago if you asked me the same question, I would have said the devil's persecution for sure. Now though, I see that many of the people that came my way in the past were also allowed by God to underline the state of my heart, or what was beneath the surface of my spiritual activities. I was okay on the outside. I thought I was holy, loving, caring, pure, sacrificial, humble, patient and gentle; all of these were on the outside. The side of me that people knew was perfect and I completely believed it. People told me I was better than them, what else did I need? That meant I was good!

But God, being purposeful, did not leave me as I was. He sent me people either to tempt me or to stress me. My first reactions were to fight the devil that sent them. Over time I began to see a pattern in my thoughts and behaviors that was different from what I thought of me. God had allowed these experiences to expose the content of my heart to me. Due to the way I responded to many of those people, I realized that I was not as holy, humble, sacrificial, patient...or any of the things I thought I was. That was when I began to question my personal relationship with Christ.

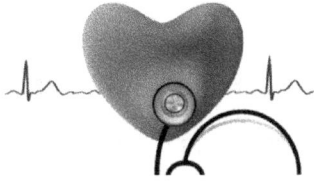

3

Look Beneath The Surface

Consider a person who goes to the hospital with headaches. There are so many pills that the doctor could prescribe to remove the pain. She may come back home with a prescription medicine that completely removes the pain, but does it really? What is the source of the pain in the first place?

It's important in our walk with God to look beneath the surface. To look deeper than what is on the outside. This brings me to the concept of living from the inside out. This is what I call a new look at the savior. As you read this, please allow God to take you deep into your own heart for a thorough look. He would love a chance to fill you completely if you will allow him.

Have you ever ventured on a journey to a place you avoided before? Picture something as easy as cleaning a closet that has been in a deserted state for years or something as difficult as going back to see someone you lied to when you were a teenager. Depending on your level of grace these tasks might be a bit difficult to complete.

At this point I must say that this is not going to be an easy task. You might be facing some things on the road that you would want to simply cover up and run away from. You might prefer to not open some doors because of the fear of where it would take you. You might even find it hard to believe that all these things are inside you. However I plead with you to trust that God will do some deep cleaning on the inside.

Therefore, having these promises, beloved, let us cleanse ourselves from all filthiness of the flesh and spirit, perfecting holiness in the fear of God. 2 Corinthians 7:1 NKJV

God has called us as Christians to a new life, the kind that brings God's grace into action daily. God has called us to look deep, to consider every single thing on the inside that can taint his glory or hide his fullness.

I have been crucified with Christ...; it is no longer I who live, but Christ... lives in me; and the life I now live in the body I live by faith in (by adherence to and reliance on and complete trust in) the Son of God, Who loved me and gave Himself up for me. Galatians 2: 20 AMP

Christ died for our sins, but that's not all. When He died, we died with him. He has given us a new life of holiness. God is able to complete what he started within us. However we have a part to play in the process.

The process of looking within will require you to allow God into every corner of your heart. How do you do this? Take a look at some of your recent interactions with people in your life; your family members, your colleagues at work, or your friends in general. What did you feel or think after these interactions? For some it's easier to live a holy life as long as there are no interactions with others.

When you go on a personal retreat, you will hardly have a clash with anyone. You are there alone with God, who is around to quarrel or argue with? But when you have to deal with conflicting viewpoints, rebuttals and criticisms, you risk the chance of a fight. Sometimes the issue here might be an external fight where you argue with someone and it may also be your thoughts about the whole interaction.

Deep cleaning sometimes seems unnecessary because we have not opened the door to see what is within. As soon as you begin the process, you better keep at it or it might be even more difficult the next time to make an attempt.

When I kept silent, my bones wasted away through my groaning all day long. For day and night your hand was heavy upon me; my strength was sapped as in the heat of summer. Then I acknowledged my sin to you and did not cover up my iniquity. I said, "I will confess my transgressions to the LORD"— and you forgave the guilt of my sin. **Psalm 32:3-5**

Prior to the work that Jesus came to do on earth; David realized the importance of allowing God into every area of his life. He knew that first acknowledging his wrong was necessary, then confessing with the aim of turning away from sin and then comes forgiveness. Many Christians today have not received forgiveness for their sin. Even though God has given them freedom from sin, they continue to live with the shame and guilt of sin.

For God is working in you, giving you the desire and the power to do what pleases him. Philippians 2:13 NLT

I want to assure you with the hope in Christ that if you will allow God to work within you, you will be free from the shame of guilt of your sins. It is God's grace that has made me free from my past and that is why I share this with you.

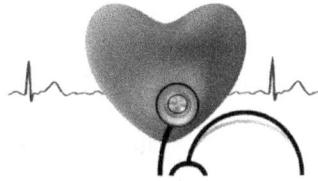

4

What Are You Looking For

The thief's purpose is to steal and kill and destroy.
My purpose is to give them a rich and satisfying
life. John 10:10. NLT

When you look deep inside do you see Christ's rich and satisfying life in all your relationships, especially the closest ones to you? For example: if you are married do you think your relationship with your spouse is rich as far as it lies within you?

Choose one of those recent interactions. Ask

yourself this question: what am I feeling on the inside towards this person? Are you angry, frustrated, sad, or are you at peace with them? Why are those feelings there? Could this be because of fear, shame or pain? Don't give up yet.

What you should be looking for is any kind of feeling that is not peaceful and joyful. Many times the feelings and thoughts are there because of some other underlying problems.

Everything that happens to you daily will bring you to either of the points in this scripture. Either to give you a rich and satisfying life or to steal and kill your joy and peace - in other words makes you feel unworthy, makes you feel like a fool, makes you see life as uninteresting and people as mean. It may even make you feel like going away from some people. It's true that some people are more difficult than others but the aim of the enemy is nothing but to make you lose sight of God's plan of abundant life.

You need to know the advantage of enjoying abundant life from Jesus Christ. You need to cultivate the habit of living from the inside out. Do you agree that it's not good enough that you are doing very well on the outside? You sing in the Choir (I know Choir members are always picked on), or you are in charge of a ministry in your church, or you may even be a pastor's wife or be in full time ministry. These do not guarantee that your life is rich and satisfying.

Guard your heart above all else, for it determines the course of your life. Proverbs 4: 23 NLT

Just as vital signs are an important test at the hospital, so too is it an important test for any Christian. It's a major spiritual test. High blood pressure is a sign of some anomaly in the heart and if it's not checked it could wreak major havoc in the body. Check your heart. If you want to really enjoy your new life in Christ and daily live a rich and satisfying life, you need to look deep within.

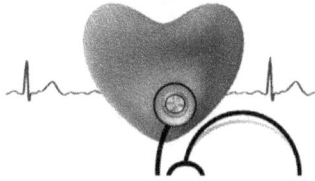

5

Your Vision

Everyone has his or her own picture of God and life. The way we see life determines what we see in life. In my personal walk as a pastor and a friend, I have come to firmly believe that if you can have a clear understanding of how God sees you; your chances are higher at living in peace.

How does God see you?

In order to help you in this area I would love to ask you some questions that will point you in the right direction. First, imagine that God is staring at you right now. How do you think He sees you?

I have asked this question to ladies while I have been counseling over the years and many times the answer I get is heart breaking. I don't know what your own candid answer is. Are you like the lady who said:

Olu you don't know how bad I have been, all the wrong things I have done in my past. And God has been there to warn me each time but I chose to not worry about him but did what I wanted. For sure God sees me as a bad girl that will never listen. He is most likely looking for another way to bring some more trouble into my life now in order to show me who I am.

Many Christians are living with the shame of their sins. They still feel the guilt like it happened yesterday, so they are not able to see God as their father. Even though God is there waiting for them to come back and enjoy His fatherly love. God's love to us is unconditional.

God is not waiting for you to repent before He can love you. He has loved you with a perfect and everlasting love. However, I believe no matter how much I try; I will not be able to convince you that God loves you. No one can convince me that another person loves me. I have to hang out with the person to know that they do.

When I met my husband, Ade, I did not need someone to tell me that he loved me. Each day since the day we became friends, I have continued to be more and more convinced that he loves me and I can respond to his love that way. Even for those that get introduced through an arranged marriage, after the first introduction, if they continue to love each other, each partner would not need a third party to explain their love.

That brings me to another major point in living from the inside out: you need to have a relationship with God. Many great people have explained having a relationship with God in different ways. And depending on the way you see life and God, I am sure you also have an explanation. As I said in the introduction, every Christian must pursue a relationship with Jesus because of their need for Him. You must ask yourself a question: do I need Him enough to pursue Him daily?

So that they should seek God, in the hope that they might feel after Him and find Him, although He is not far from each one of us, Acts 17:27 AMP.

Come close to God, and God will come close to you. Wash your hands, you sinners; purify your hearts, for your loyalty is divided between God and the world. James 4: 8 NLT

God wants you to seek Him. He has promised to draw near when you draw near to him. Your perspective on life and your views about God will change daily as you form a fellowship with Him.

You will also begin to see Him in a new way. There are so many tools that have been developed to help you know God. The bible is the most important of them all. If you approach the bible with a determination to know God, you will definitely find him.

There is no greater tool out there that could help you understand who God is than the bible. There are so many great Christian books, so many sermons have been preached and so many Christian blogs written that would bless you, all attempting to direct you to God. The Bible is like a mirror which also gives you access to the kingdom of God. As a mirror it helps you see who you are and what Christ has made you. It also shows you the difference between the truth and some lies you have believed about yourself and about life.

For the word of God is alive and powerful. It is sharper than the sharpest two-edged sword, cutting between soul and spirit, between joint and marrow. It exposes our innermost thoughts and desires. Hebrews 4:12 NLT

I encourage you to venture into studying the word of God. I find that as a young believer it was easier to read the Old Testament than the new because it has more stories. So I started reading the Old Testament and I would read until I got to a point where I did not understand what is being said.

However, when I changed the way of studying the bible from knowing more stories of the bible to knowing that God of the Bible, I began to love and understand reading the New Testament. I wanted to know what Jesus really did for me.

The first book I really studied was Romans. By the time I was in the sixth chapter, I was full of joy. I became so sure that God loves me. I got to know the confidence of being a daughter of the Most High.

If you don't know anything about Christ I advise

that you start with the gospels: Matthew, Mark, Luke, and John; then read what happened after Jesus left. Read this with the mind of knowing how God sees you.

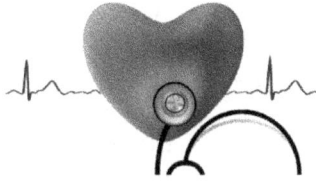

6

How Do You See Yourself?

My next question to you is 'when you look at yourself what do you see?' Are you one of those superstars in our world today with breathtaking beauty and a figure that every lady desires? Are you exceptional at arts and crafts? Are you a straight A student? Are you the best cook in your circle of friends? Are you gifted with all kinds of great gifts? Or are you none of the above?

Many of us are average and ordinary but we grow

up seeing some highly talented people, and we go all-out to become like them. We venture into business, sports, arts to do it exceptionally and in many cases fail to shine. Because of this we change the way we see ourselves. There are so many people walking around today that are convinced that they are failures. After all they can't find anything in their lives to boast about.

Are you one of those people who are mad at God for not giving you such and such gifts? How long did it take you to agree that you would stop trying to be another person? Many keep chasing other people's dreams only to become more frustrated than when they first began.

Let me tell you here that you are wrong. Yes, you may be ordinary, and guess what: God made you ordinary. He is looking forward to you coming to him just as you are so that He may breathe His grace into your life to bring forth what He wants of you.

Have you noticed when you go to church and listen to sermons encouraging you to believe God loves you, that you may walk in this knowledge for a few days only to lose confidence again the next day?

Sermons are not there to be your main source of connection to God. You need God himself to talk to you often enough.

When you see such a scripture as Philippians 4:13, what comes to mind?

I have strength for all things in Christ who empowers me [I am ready for anything and equal to anything through Him who infuses inner strength into me; I am self-sufficient in Christ's sufficiency]. Philippians 4:13 AMP

Do you see God's help in your life? Do you agree that He would help you do all He wants you to do? If God made you in His own image, forming every detail of your system, I believe He can also strengthen you in any area of life that He directs you to. After you have accepted who He made you, and the way He planned your life, then you will also need to be open to Him helping you.

Many people are able to follow God and love Him except if He asks them to do one thing or another. For example: some are willing to help the poor as long as God doesn't ask them to be poor. Some are willing to lead at Church except if he would tell them to be on the same team with that other person who cheated on them. Whatever God has called you to do; He infuses strength into you daily to do it too. It is for His glory.

God sometimes wants to stretch your ability when He asks you to do certain things. Do you feel He is challenging you to enter into a place you cannot handle? Maybe it's because He is the only one that can sustain you? Then trust Him. It is for His glory. Don't hide or run from God. He wants to build your faith.

I remember that when we started Overcomers Assembly, I thought in my head, "of course I can do it. After all, I have been involved with my older brother's ministry in Nigeria. I am sure it's going to be easy. I am experienced". I didn't know that God was requiring much more from me. He was going to bring me to a place that I had never been to in my whole life.

He brought some very difficult situations and people my way. Many times I wanted to run and sometimes I wanted to deal with things my way; many times I even tried to help Him since I thought He was too slow. But I either failed or He did not allow me to succeed. All the while He kept transforming me.

I remember the day I learned that a church member had lied about me to another person. I really wanted to prove myself right and them wrong but the Lord had another option. He wanted to show his love to the people involved. He also wanted to show me that it doesn't matter what people think or say about me; what He thinks is the most important opinion.

Another time I got home to find a letter on my door from someone disappointed that I did not meet their own expectations as a pastor's wife. Though I was hurt, I got to see that being what God called me to be was more important than having good favor with others.

You will be able to do all that God would ask you. You might be terrified and scared but He will give you strength on a daily basis. He has promised that if you do your part of the deal of coming to listen daily, He will do His part and a vibrant life will be the result.

I must say here that I have not attained perfection and I still struggle with many of the issues I face daily, but I have learned to surrender to His every word or at least work hard to surrender daily.

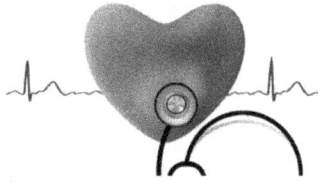

7

Are You Thirsty Enough?

"Is anyone thirsty? Come and drink— even if you have no money! Come, take your choice of wine or milk— it's all free! Why spend your money on food that does not give you strength? Why pay for food that does you no good? Listen to me, and you will eat what is good. You will enjoy the finest food.

"Come to me with your ears wide open. Listen and you will find life. I will make an everlasting covenant with you. I will give you all the unfailing love I promised to David. See how I used him to

display my power among the peoples. I made him a leader among the nations. You also will command nations you do not know, and peoples unknown to you will come running to obey, because I, the Lord your God, the Holy One of Israel, have made you glorious."

Seek the Lord while you can find him. Call on him now while he is near. Let the wicked change their ways and banish the very thought of doing wrong. Let them turn to the Lord that he may have mercy on them. Yes, turn to our God, for he will forgive generously.

"My thoughts are nothing like your thoughts," says the Lord. "And my ways are far beyond anything you could imagine. For just as the heavens are higher than the earth, so my ways are higher than your ways and my thoughts higher than your thoughts.

"The rain and snow come down from the heavens

and stay on the ground to water the earth. They cause the grain to grow, producing seed for the farmer and bread for the hungry. It is the same with my word. I send it out, and it always produces fruit. It will accomplish all I want it to, and it will prosper everywhere I send it. You will live in joy and peace. The mountains and hills will burst into song, and the trees of the field will clap their hands! Where once there were thorns, cypress trees will grow. Where nettles grew, myrtles will sprout up.

These events will bring great honor to the Lord's name; they will be an everlasting sign of his power and love." Isaiah 55: 1-13 NLT

Living from the inside out requires being thirsty. The Merriam-Webster dictionary defines thirst as **an uncomfortable feeling that is caused by the need for something to drink, a very great need for something to drink, a strong desire for something, deficient in moisture.** Are you thirsty? Do you feel uncomfortable about your current state? And is it causing you to sense a great need for Christ's kind of life?

If you are thirsty then here is a call for you. The God that we serve is a loving God. He has made provision for each one of us in Jesus Christ. No matter what your background is, no matter what your past is like. Just come. There is fulfillment for your soul. Come and drink.

You might have spent your life on some relationship that did not end up well. You might have wasted your time and are in a place today that you wish you were not. If you are thirsty for a rich life, if you want a real change, you need to get busy. God's call to you today is to come and drink.

Come with your ears wide open to receive life. God is the only one that can give you unconditional and true love and He is calling you to that now. The reason you are in this place now is because you might have been looking for unconditional love from people. No one can give that except through God.

If you are thirsty and you look into the word of God you will discover the way that God deals with His own people, those that are sold out to Him. He cares for them. You will begin to see how much you mean to God.

Fruitfulness, peace, joy and passion will be added to your life as you seek the Lord daily. Then your confidence will rest upon him. Then you will walk around with no worries of what tomorrow will bring. As the prince or princess of the most high you have no need to worry, but that can only happen if you develop a solid relationship with your father, the king.

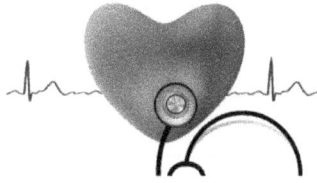

8

Your Thoughts And Feelings

Guard your heart above all else for it determines the course of your life. Proverbs 4:23 NLT

Your thoughts also create some feelings. Fear is one of the greatest sources of negative feelings. Do you get angry with people around you? Could this be as a result of fear?

Fear is a major plague in the life of a man or woman. There are so many "what-ifs". I worked in financial planning for many years and I discovered early in my career that many people are living in fear as living dead. Fear of critical illness, disability, death, insufficient funds and need for long term care. Insurance is a good product, just as investments are. However buying the insurance product does not take away your fears. You will still need to deal with them.

I used to be crippled with fear as well. I used to wonder what would happen to my family if I was dead. And this kind of thought creates others like it. The enemy wants to keep you bound in your way of thinking. He knows he can continue to control you as long as He can keep you focused on the 'what ifs'. I have found a better way of living: teach your spirit to learn to say No!

Say No to the negative thoughts in your own head. Don't allow negative thoughts to be in charge of your life. Whether you are busy or idle, your mind is busy working. Some of the thoughts that go through the mind on any given day could be negative, depressing and fearful. You need to train yourself to catch these negative thoughts and choose not to spend your day thinking this way.

You may need to talk back to your thoughts as if you are talking to someone younger than you. Tell your thoughts to stop. There is no need wasting the whole day on negative thoughts when you could be thinking about positive things about yourself and about life in general.

Summing it all up, friends, I'd say you'll do best by filling your minds and meditating on things true, noble, reputable, authentic, compelling, gracious—the best, not the worst; the beautiful, not the ugly; things to praise, not things to curse. Put into practice what you learned from me, what you heard and saw and realized. Do that, and God, who makes everything work together, will work you into his most excellent harmonies. Philippians 4:8-9 MSG

Say No also to people who wants to use your fears to control you. God made us for His own pleasure; He made us to need Him. There is a longing inside of us for more that only God can satisfy. However, sometimes pleasing people around us especially the ones we respect can make us feel happy. This makes it hard to say no when these people come up with projects they want us to do.

However, if you keep saying yes to people around you, you won't have a life. Saying yes could increase your level of excitements but could end in frustration. You may feel good helping everyone around you but what good is it if it is not what God has planned for you?

Learn to say yes only to God, and "No!" to everything else as long as it does not fit into the plan that God has set for you. You must account for your time here when you stand before God in heaven; I think it's important to do only what would count.

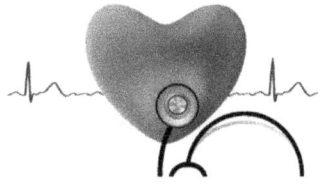

9

Your Body

I was looking at myself in the mirror one day when the Lord spoke to me. Have you ever taken time to thank me for each and every part of your body? And of course my response to God was no. He wanted to underline the way I thought about my body. I never used to like some parts of my body.

I grew up wishing my teeth were set in a different way and therefore that my mouth would look different. But on this certain day I confronted my ingratitude and took the opportunity to begin celebrating my frame. God then asked me this:

"who determines what is beautiful?"

You think about it for a while. You know what you wish you were like; who says this is the best look? Hollywood, your culture, and your environment; not God! At that point in my life I had made up my mind to live according to the word of God and nothing else. And seeing that I had been living on the world's expectations was mind-boggling. I repented of my sin of ingratitude and made up my mind to see my body differently.

It took a while to love every part, especially the ones I had issues with. You may ask what this has to do with living from the inside out. A lot! We live in a world that is centered on living from the outside. You walk into the mall and you will see what I mean.

Every company in there is promising you a better life if only you would buy their products. You will have the perfect look with this lipstick. Your life will be fabulous if only you use this hair product. You will have fulfillment in life if only you would open an account with us.

The aim is to make you focus on what you want: the looks, the style, the happiness, and the class - the kind of life that you want. However, living from the inside out is the opposite of that. You focus on what is on the inside; you check what you are thinking about, not what you see.

We see a model on the cover of a magazine and think she is so lovely; however, in some cases, she doesn't think the same. She is constantly looking for meaning in life. She thinks her life is empty. Not only that, she also has a fear of losing her job the moment another hot girl comes along.

Some of the people that determine the way you see yourself don't like their own lives. But you see them as lucky. You see them as lovely while they see themselves as hopeless.

What is your vision of yourself? How do you see your body? When you see yourself in the mirror, what do you see? Do you see someone wonderfully and fearfully made? Do you see God's image? If God made you in his own image, why do you keep looking down on yourself?

Many people today see themselves as disadvantaged because they are like this or like that. Not only that, they hate the other type of people. They say things like: "you are lucky you are like this." They don't understand why you still complain if you have what they want. The way you see yourself will determine the way you see other people.

In order to switch from 'living from the outside in' to 'living from the inside out' as it concerns your body, the next time you are in front of a mirror, look at yourself and consider if there is any part that you would have loved to change and ask yourself why you feel that way. Then see if there is any ingratitude there, like it was for me, and repent from the way you were thinking.

Make up your mind to work hard on seeing your body as the image of God. As you do, you will learn to package yourself beautifully. I learned this as a young girl. My mom always talks about your packaging. If you are giving someone a gift, they would appreciate it better if it's elegantly wrapped. So package yourself daily in the way you would love your gifts to be packaged. And if you have been treating your body in a wrong way, you also need to repent and allow God to show you your value. Then you can learn how to treat your body as God's image.

The more you focus on God's word the more you will see yourself as a gift to this planet. As you continue to be transformed in your thought of who you are, as you discover the value that God has placed on you in Christ, your value for yourself will begin to catch up to God's.

Living from the inside out is living a rich and abundant life. It's available to you and you can enjoy it if only you pursue Christ intimately and allow him in every area of your life.

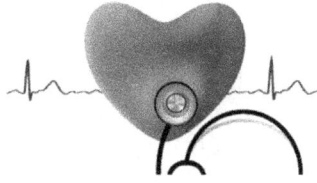

10

Your Words Becomes His Word

As you focus on God's words, your thoughts begin to align with His word, your faith will rise and you will begin to operate based on what you believe and not on your worries and fears.

It is written, "I have made you a father of many nations." God considers Abraham to be our father. The God that Abraham believed in gives life to the dead. Abraham's God also speaks of things that do not exist as if they do exist. Romans 4:17 NIRV

What happened to Abraham is about to happen to you. In the introduction I explained the false change that many people pretend to have. That type of change does not come from the inside out. This is the opposite of that.

As you spend time with God, be becomes real to you and you begin to have the faith of Him. Just like Abraham, you begin to believe whatever the Lord speaks to you. He no longer is just a God but He becomes your rock and fortress. He becomes your strength.

This God is the one that called into existence everything that we see today out of nothing. He formed the moon and the stars. He created the living things and every single planet there is. And all these He made from nothing. As you hang out with God you begin to think like Him.

The spiritual will become obvious to you. You no longer see your limitations; you no longer see the walls that you have put up as you grew in life. You begin to see with the eyes of faith. You begin to see the good in everyone and every situation.

Loving people will seem easy to you because you now have access to the grace of God. You won't feel the pressure of getting approval from others because you are sure of His approval. And then your words will begin to align to His will. This cannot happen in a day. It will take time to renew your mind. However, it will happen for sure if you get busy from now on.

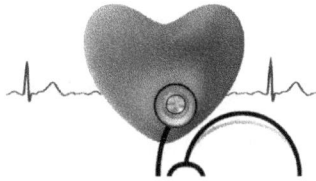

11

Your Life, Your Age, Your Relationship

Gray hair is a crown of glory; it is gained by living a godly life. Proverbs 16:31 NLT

Many women are not happy, as they grow older. They have lots of regret. They keep wishing they could be young again. Some focus solely on the wrinkles, and they envy or even look down on the younger ladies.

Some mothers become jealous of their teenage daughter's looks. "That used to be me," they say.

They find something wrong with everyone that looks younger than them. They think in their mind that no one understands their situation. When they see someone that has the lives they desired they are mean to the person.

This also happen in the workplace. There is competition. Everyone is trying to prove to be the best, backbiting about others and bashing each other. As you get busy renewing your mind, you begin to see life differently. You will no longer look down on who you are.

Teach us to realize the brevity of life, so that we may grow in wisdom. Psalms 90:12 NLT

When you hang out with God, you receive His grace for the past and you begin to enjoy every day of your life. You accept the love of God that fully covers all your faults in the past and trust Him to teach you how to live today.

Relationship

Everyone longs to be understood and valued so we do everything possible to be noticed and respected. We forget most times that we were all made to need each other. A girl wants her parent's attention and time so much that she forgets that the parents need her as well. A wife wants her husband to appreciate her so bad that she forgets he wants the same.

Living from the inside out will require that you begin to look at every relationship in your life differently. If you were the kind that put your needs over others consider thinking about other people's needs too. Also make up your mind to allow people in your life do only what they have been designed to do.

Some people get married and think that their main duty in their spouse's life is to change them and they get busy doing just that. An important fact is that men were made differently than women. If a woman begins to teach a man how to be a man and vice verse, I think they might be attempting to give what they don't have.

This kind of situation in marriage brings so much frustration. Men are wired differently than women. Some men are more organized than their wives and some women are more structured than their husbands. It will be really frustrating to consider changing your spouse to think like you. If there is something you don't like the way your spouse handles, it's important to give them the freedom to change on their own terms not yours.

A prudent person foresees danger and takes precautions. The simpleton goes blindly on and suffers the consequences. Proverbs 27:12 NLT

As you learn to live from the inside out, you will learn to be considerate of other people. You stop seeing things as if you are the only wise person in existence. You learn caution as it applies to your relationships.

My dear brothers and sisters take note of this: Everyone should be quick to listen, slow to speak and slow to become angry, James 1:19 NIV

You listen to the Holy Spirit for when to talk and when to be silent. Of course this is a process. It won't all happen in a day. In other words you will still make mistakes, but if you keep coming back to God, He will keep working on transforming you. You will learn how to love like God. Living from the inside out will enrich your relationships.

And God showed his love for us by sending his only Son into the world, so that we might have life through him. 1John 4:9 GNT

You now have life through Jesus. He came to give you abundant life. Christ did not come to save you only from eternal death; He also came to give you a full and satisfying life. In order words, you are able to live and love like Jesus. If only you will submit to His daily working in you.

The point here not to learn a new kind of behavior; what you need to do it to live in union with God. What does it mean to live in union with God? You live based on his leading and instructions to you every single moment. You give him access to your heart. You do nothing without him. When this happens, you will begin to live an abundant life through Christ. You will begin to love like Christ.

Dear friends, let us love one another, because love comes from God. Whoever loves is a child of God and knows God. Whoever does not love does not know God, for God is love. And God showed his love for us by sending his only Son into the world, so that we might have life through him. This is what love is: it is not that we have loved God, but that he loved us and sent his Son to be the means by which our sins are forgiven. Dear friends, if this is how God loved us, then we should love one another. No one has ever seen God, but if we love one another, God lives in union with us, and his love is made perfect in us. We are sure that we live in union with God and that he lives in union with us, because he has given us his Spirit. And we have seen and tell others that the Father sent his Son to be the Savior of the world. If we declare that Jesus is the Son of God, we live in union with God and God lives in union with us. And we ourselves know and believe the love which God has for us.

God is love, and those who live in love live in union with God and God lives in union with them. Love is made perfect in us in order that we may have courage on the Judgment Day; and we will have it because our life in this world is the same as Christ's. There is no fear in love; perfect love drives out all fear. So then, love has not been made perfect in anyone who is afraid, because fear has to do with punishment. We love because God first loved us. If we say we love God, but hate others, we are liars. For we cannot love God, whom we have not seen, if we do not love others, whom we have seen. The command that Christ has given us is this: whoever loves God must love others also. 1 John 4: 7-21

Therefore, let Christ's abundant life affect each of your relationships.

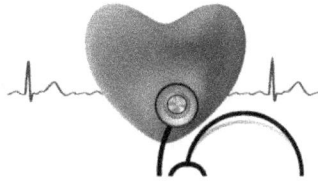

12

Ought To Pray And Not To Faint

And he spake a parable unto them to this end, that men ought always to pray, and not to faint. Luke 18:1 KJV

It was another busy week and I had become really tired. My body was weak, my mind was stressed, I was easily irritable and I can say I was fainting (physically and spiritually) as I put the boys to bed. I was just about to excuse myself from their room when they asked that I stayed a little longer with them.

I had planned to spend some extra time in prayers knowing the state of things and the schedule I still have after their bed time. Therefore when they asked for more of my time I had to tell them I needed to pray. Demi said "you can pray here" and his brother was in full support. I explained to them that I needed to pray out loud this time and might disturb them but they insisted and said they would love me to pray in their room.

So I lay in bed with them and I began to pray. It was a very beautiful experience because as I prayed they prayed. (What started that day is still in practice today). Meanwhile, I woke up from their bed about 30 minutes later really refreshed while they were sound asleep.

Why did I share that? After I woke up that day I got a new understanding of what The Lord Jesus meant when He said men ought always to pray and not to faint.

I was fainting; spirit, soul and body but a little rest and prayers revived me. This experience taught me to regularly check for any sign of tiredness in my body to see if it also indicates that I am fainting. Looking into my heart had been a vital part of my Christian walk and now I realized that body weakness is also a sign to look for.

Fainting in Jesus' statement could mean anything at different points in life to different people. Merriam-Webster Dictionary describes **faint as: to lose courage or spirit, to become weak.** In a real world there is stress coming from different issues. And stress can cause one to faint physically and emotionally.

Your best practice is to deal with this when it's still in the heart. How will you know when you are at this point? Check your heart regularly or plan to do a check during your daily devotion time in the morning or at night. If you see fear, disappointments, anger, resentments, hatred, guilt, or any feeling that is not from God's spirit. You know that you are fainting.

What that means is that you are struggling to sustain your life in Christ. Jesus gave you His life and at this moment you are losing air. You need Him now than ever before.

However in this state you could also begin to see other people as the cause of your stress. As much as this could be true you are responsible for the way you chose to react towards the pressures you might be getting.

Spend extra time in prayers especially the moment you catch your heart fainting. Submit your heart to God as you pray. And make up your mind to rid your heart of any of these feelings. As I pray, the easy way out usually for me is to meditate on God's words that relates to what I am feeling.

Then the Holy Spirit opens my heart to see the situations in a clearer way. He also gives me the grace I need to do what God words say. Then I choose to let go of my rights and my pains, I choose to forgive if needed and I choose to understand with others. I stay in prayers until my heart is free of the negative feelings. Sometimes this goes on for days, I keep dealing with my heart until all is cleared or let me say I stay dependent on His grace every hour.

Someone may argue that it's not important to focus on your negative feelings. No, don't focus on them, let God get rid of them. Negative thoughts can ruin you. Negative thought that is not dealt with leads to negative actions that can destroy a person's life. For example; fear can create a void that leaves the person sensitive to others people's behaviors which can then cause offense, then anger then resentments and then hatred the list goes on which can eventually lead to assault or even murder. Yes this is exaggerated, but you get the point. Deal with negative feelings before they destroy you.

There is grace in prayer. Receive it daily. Don't faint! Live a joyful life in Christ. Remember that you no longer live, you are dead and Christ lives in you. Let Him control your heart. Let him maintain your joy level; let him fill you to overflowing with His peace that brings rest in every area of life.

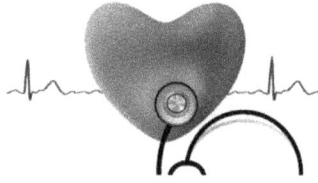

Conclusion

And set your minds and keep them set on what is above (the higher things), not on the things that are on the earth. Colossians 3:2 AMP

Real change is possible but it requires a change in your mentality. Your thinking is what makes you act the way you do. The reason you have not been able to change might be because you have been changing the wrong thing. What are you focused on? What are you watching? What are you reading? What are you thinking about? Change is not coming if you don't set your mind on the things of God and His ways.

Guard your heart above all else for it determines the course of your life. Proverbs 4:23 NLT

Every single mistake I have ever made in life was tied to my way of thinking. No one just does things without thinking it first, whether consciously or otherwise. The last 5, 10, 20 years have been a product of your thoughts. The next 5, 10, 20 years will be a product of your thoughts.

You are who you are today because of the way you have been thinking to date. You might have missed out on life and some of good stuffs. You might have thought that no one cares about you or that you are different. If that's true then it's possible that is why you have not experienced the joy of the Lord so far.

Remember that your future will be dependent on the way you think from now on. Look around you, at your life and your relatives. Where are the people around you? Is there anyone thriving in their lives? Are they displaying the glory of God? Think about it. Their way of thinking has brought them to this point in their lives.

Would you desire to be in a place where God can display His light through you? A place of great peace and joy. A place where you thrive loving your live because you continually glorify God?

Don't copy the behavior and customs of this world, but let God transform you into a new person by changing the way you think. Then you will learn to know God's will for you, who is good and pleasing and perfect. Romans 12:2 NLT

Here is a new project for you. I challenge you to subject your mind to the word of God and He will begin to change the way you think. As you get busy at this process of renewing your mind, He will get busy molding a new you. The Lord will help you but you must work hard at submitting to all His corrections.

Because of the privilege and authority God has given me, I give each of you this warning: Don't think you are better than you really are. Be honest in your evaluation of yourselves, measuring yourselves by the faith God has given us Romans 12: 3 NLT

In his grace, God has given us different gifts for doing certain things well. So if God has given you the ability to prophesy, speak out with as much faith as God has given you. Romans 12:6 NLT

You need to locate what he designed you for. Many have shipwrecked their lives by trying to be like another person. If you can stay in line with the word of God and keep subjecting your thinking to it day and night, you will be able to learn what the will of God is for you. No one earns a degree unless they go through the process of learning. You need to subject yourself to the word of God.

Learn to think the way He designed you to think.

Just as you feed your body daily, feed your spirit also. Connect yourself to a living Church of God and connect yourself to a small group where you can find other believers that are walking in line with the word of God. They will help you to prove that you are in God's will. They will love and correct you when needed. Don't run away from their relationship. Work hard together with people that love you. Remember that they are humans like you and though they might have grown, they also have the same needs like you do.

Every single one of us can shine as vessels in the hands of God. We can do what He has called us and graced us to do. Get busy today with the renewing of your mind and you will begin to live from the inside out.

No one gets a degree by going to school for the first 3 weeks of the semester. You have to finish strong. That is why you need to always surround yourself with people that you can be accountable to.

God bless you.

Endnotes

Introduction
John 10:10: Amplified Bible (AMP)
Copyright © 1954, 1958, 1962, 1964, 1965, 1987 by The Lockman Foundation

Look beneath the surface
2 Corinthians 7:1 New King James Version (NKJV)
The Holy Bible, New King James Version. Copyright © 1982 by Thomas Nelson, Inc.

Galatians 2:20
Amplified Bible (AMP)
Copyright © 1954, 1958, 1962, 1964, 1965, 1987 by The Lockman Foundation

Psalm 32:3-5
New International Version (NIV)
Holy Bible, New International Version®, NIV® Copyright © 1973, 1978, 1984, 2011 by Biblica, Inc.® Used by permission. All rights reserved worldwide.

Philippians 2:13 NLT
New Living Translation (NLT)
Holy Bible. New Living Translation copyright© 1996, 2004, 2007 by Tyndale House Foundation. Used by permission of Tyndale House Publishers Inc., Carol Stream, Illinois 60188. All rights reserved.

What are you looking for?
John 10:10.
New Living Translation (NLT)
Holy Bible. New Living Translation copyright© 1996, 2004, 2007 by Tyndale House Foundation. Used by permission of Tyndale House Publishers Inc., Carol Stream, Illinois 60188. All rights reserved.

Proverbs 4: 23
New Living Translation (NLT)
Holy Bible. New Living Translation copyright© 1996, 2004, 2007 by Tyndale House Foundation. Used by permission of Tyndale House Publishers Inc., Carol Stream, Illinois 60188. All rights reserved.

Your Vision
Acts 17:27
Amplified Bible (AMP)
Copyright © 1954, 1958, 1962, 1964, 1965, 1987 by The Lockman Foundation

James 4: 8
New Living Translation (NLT)
Holy Bible. New Living Translation copyright© 1996, 2004, 2007 by Tyndale House Foundation. Used by permission of Tyndale House Publishers Inc., Carol Stream, Illinois 60188. All rights reserved.

Hebrews 4:12
New Living Translation (NLT)
Holy Bible. New Living Translation copyright© 1996, 2004, 2007 by Tyndale House Foundation. Used by permission of Tyndale House Publishers Inc., Carol Stream, Illinois 60188. All rights reserved.

How do you see yourself?
Philippians 4:13
Amplified Bible (AMP)
Copyright © 1954, 1958, 1962, 1964, 1965, 1987 by The Lockman Foundation

Are you Thirsty
Isaiah 55:
New Living Translation (NLT)
Holy Bible. New Living Translation copyright© 1996, 2004, 2007 by Tyndale House Foundation. Used by permission of Tyndale

House Publishers Inc., Carol Stream, Illinois 60188. All rights reserved.

"Thirst." Merriam-Webster.com. Merriam-Webster, n.d. Web. 9 Apr. 2014.
http://www.merriam-webster.com/dictionary/thirst

Your Thoughts and feelings
Philippians 4:8-9
The Message (MSG)
Copyright © 1993, 1994, 1995, 1996, 2000, 2001, 2002 by Eugene H. Peterson

Proverbs 4:23
New Living Translation (NLT)
Holy Bible. New Living Translation copyright© 1996, 2004, 2007 by Tyndale House Foundation. Used by permission of Tyndale House Publishers Inc., Carol Stream, Illinois 60188. All rights reserved.

Your words becomes His word
Romans 4:17
New International Reader's Version (NIRV)
Copyright © 1996, 1998 by Biblica

Your life, your age you relationship
Proverbs 16:31
New Living Translation (NLT)
Holy Bible. New Living Translation copyright© 1996, 2004, 2007 by Tyndale House Foundation. Used by permission of Tyndale House Publishers Inc., Carol Stream, Illinois 60188. All rights reserved.

Psalms 90:12
New Living Translation (NLT)
Holy Bible. New Living Translation copyright© 1996, 2004, 2007 by Tyndale House Foundation. Used by permission of Tyndale House Publishers Inc., Carol Stream, Illinois 60188. All rights reserved.

Proverbs 27:12
New Living Translation (NLT)
Holy Bible. New Living Translation copyright© 1996, 2004, 2007 by Tyndale House Foundation. Used by permission of Tyndale House Publishers Inc., Carol Stream, Illinois 60188. All rights reserved.

James 1:19
New International Version (NIV)
Holy Bible, New International Version®, NIV® Copyright © 1973, 1978, 1984, 2011 by Biblica, Inc.® Used by permission. All rights reserved worldwide.

1John 4:7-21
Good News Translation (GNT)
Copyright © 1992 by American Bible Society

Ought to Pray and not to faint
Luke 18:1
King James Version (KJV)
By Public Domain

"Faint." Merriam-Webster.com. Merriam-Webster, n.d. Web. 10 Apr. 2014.
http://www.merriam-webster.com/dictionary/faint.

Conclusion
Colossians 3:2
Amplified Bible (AMP)
Copyright © 1954, 1958, 1962, 1964, 1965, 1987 by The Lockman Foundation

Proverbs 4:23
New Living Translation (NLT)
Holy Bible. New Living Translation copyright© 1996, 2004, 2007 by Tyndale House Foundation. Used by permission of Tyndale House Publishers Inc., Carol Stream, Illinois 60188. All rights reserved.

Romans 12:2, 3, 6
New Living Translation (NLT)
Holy Bible. New Living Translation copyright© 1996, 2004, 2007 by Tyndale House Foundation. Used by permission of Tyndale House Publishers Inc., Carol Stream, Illinois 60188. All rights reserved.

....

The principles in this book are intended to point your attention always to Jesus. For more information about

- Olu's seminars and conference schedule

- Engaging Olu as a speaker for your group

- Future books and materials

- Past and Current blog posts

Visit www.OluSobanjo.com

....

www.ingramcontent.com/pod-product-compliance
Lightning Source LLC
Chambersburg PA
CBHW021135020426
42331CB00005B/780